practical
stamp decorating
projects for home ornaments and accessories

practical stamp decorating

projects for home ornaments and accessories

Over 30 beautiful and easy-to-follow decorative stamp-painting projects for china, glass, stationery, giftwrap, picture frames, lampshades, boxes and trays • Step-by-step instructions and more than 360 colour photographs • Creative advice on making your own original stamps and mixing paints

Stewart and Sally Walton

southwater

This edition is published by Southwater

Southwater is an imprint of Anness Publishing Ltd
Hermes House, 88–89 Blackfriars Road, London SE1 8HA
tel. 020 7401 2077; fax 020 7633 9499
www.southwaterbooks.com; info@anness.com

© Anness Publishing Ltd 2006

UK agent: The Manning Partnership Ltd
6 The Old Dairy, Melcombe Road
Bath BA2 3LR; tel. 01225 478444; fax 01225 478440
sales@manning-partnership.co.uk

UK distributor: Grantham Book Services Ltd
Isaac Newton Way, Alma Park Industrial Estate
Grantham, Lincs NG31 9SD
tel. 01476 541080; fax 01476 541061
orders@gbs.tbs-ltd.co.uk

North American agent/distributor: National Book Network
4501 Forbes Boulevard, Suite 200, Lanham, MD 20706
tel. 301 459 3366; fax 301 429 5746
www.nbnbooks.com

Australian agent/distributor: Pan Macmillan Australia
Level 18, St Martins Tower, 31 Market St, Sydney, NSW 2000
tel. 1300 135 113; fax 1300 135 103
customer.service@macmillan.com.au

New Zealand agent/distributor: David Bateman Ltd
30 Tarndale Grove, Off Bush Road, Albany, Auckland
tel. (09) 415 7664; fax (09) 415 8892

A CIP catalogue record for this book is available from
the British Library.

Publisher: Joanna Lorenz
Editorial Director: Judith Simons
Editors: Felicity Forster and Elizabeth Woodland
Copy Editor: Judy Cox
Photographer: Graham Rae
Stylists: Diana Civil, Andrea Spencer and Fanny Ward
Designer: Ian Sandom
Cover Designer: Balley Design Associates
Production Controller: Claire Rae

Previously published as part of a larger volume,
The Complete Book of Decorative Stamping

1 3 5 7 9 10 8 6 4 2

CONTENTS

STAMPING BASICS

The stamp decorating idea comes from the rubber office stamp and it uses the same principle – all the equipment you will need is a stamp and some colour. Commercial stamps are readily available, but included in this book is practical advice on how to create your own stamps from wood or sponge, rubber or linoleum – almost any material that will hold colour and release it. Stamps can be used with an inkpad, but a small foam roller gives a better effect: just coat the stamp with ink or ordinary household paint – this makes stamping a fairly inexpensive option. Follow the tips on application techniques and paint effects to achieve the look best suited to your home.

ABOVE: Simple home-made or ready-made stamps, printed at different angles, make a charming alternative to machine-printed wrapping paper.

LEFT: If you have never tried stamping before, begin with a small project such as these book covers, using just one bold stamp.

CREATING STAMPS

There is a huge range of ready-made stamps to choose from, but it is also very satisfying to make your own unique stamps. The following pages show you how to make several kinds of stamp, using different materials. These are often suitable for different surfaces and uses. For example, flexible foam stamps make printing on to a curved glass surface a much easier proposition, and you can also create large shapes. Wood and lino stamps are more difficult to cut, but you may want to graduate to these once you have gained experience and confidence. A good way to begin is with the humble potato-cut. Once you have started creating your own stamps, you won't want to stop!

WOOD AND LINOLEUM STAMPS

Stamped prints were first made with carved wooden blocks. Indian textiles are still produced by hand in this way and it has recently become possible to buy traditional carved printing blocks. Designs are cut in outline and the

ABOVE: Create the effect of wood blocks (top) with handmade linocuts (bottom).

backgrounds are scooped out to leave the pattern shapes standing proud of the surface. Ink is applied, either by dipping the block or rolling colour on to the surface. The design is stamped and appears in reverse. The craft of making wooden printing blocks takes time to learn: you need special tools that are razor sharp, and an understanding about cutting with or against the grain. Practise on a bonded wood like marine plywood, which is relatively easy to carve.

Linoleum blocks are available from art and craft suppliers and usually come ready mounted in a range of sizes. Lino is a natural material made from ground cork and linseed oil on a webbed string backing. It is cut in the same way as wood, but has a less resistant texture and no grain to contend with, so is simple to cut.

To make a lino stamp you will need to trace a design and reverse the tracing before transferring it to the lino; this way you will print the design the right way around. Fill in all the background areas with a permanent marker pen: these are the parts to be scooped out, leaving the design proud of the surface. You will need at least three tools – a craft knife,

a V-shaped gouge and a scoop. All the tools should be kept as sharp as possible to make cutting easier and safer. Lino is easiest to cut when slightly warm, so place the block on a radiator for ten minutes before cutting. Hold down the block with your spare hand behind your cutting hand, then if the tool slips you will not hurt yourself.

FOAM STAMPS

Different types of foam are characterized by their density. The main types used for stamp-making in this book are: high-density foam, such as upholstery foam; medium-density sponge, such as a kitchen sponge; and low-density sponge, such as a bath sponge. The different densities of foam are each suited to a particular kind of project; on the whole, medium- or low-density sponges are best for bold solid shapes, and high-density foam for fine details. Polystyrene foam (Styrofoam) can also be used but must be mounted on to hardboard. When the glue has dried, the polystyrene can be cut through to the board and the background can be lifted, leaving the design as a stamp.

ABOVE: Home-made stamps cut from high- and medium-density foam.

RUBBER STAMPS

Rubber stamps have come out of the office and playroom and emerged as remarkable interior decorating tools. Shops have sprung up dealing exclusively in an incredible range of stamp designs and the mail-order selections are astounding. The advantage of these pre-cut stamps is that you are instantly ready to transform fabric, furniture, even walls – and there can be no quicker way to add pattern to a surface. However, rubber stamps are most suited to small projects that require fine detail.

There are two methods of creating your own rubber stamp.

The first is to design on paper and then have a rubber-stamp company make one for you. This is worth doing if you intend to make good use of the stamp, and not just use it for a small, one-off project. Custom-made stamps are quite expensive to produce, so unless money is no object you may like to consider a second option. You can also make stamps by carving your design into an ordinary eraser. Many erasers are now made of a plastic compound instead of actual rubber, but the surface is smooth and easy to cut into. The best motifs to use on these eraser stamps are small geometric shapes, which can be used to build up patterns or border designs.

To make a sponge stamp, first trace your chosen design then lightly spray the back of the pattern with adhesive, which will make it tacky but removable. Stick the pattern on to the foam and use a sharp craft knife to cut around the shape. Remove any background by cutting across to meet the outlines. If you are using medium- or low-density foam, part it after the initial outline cut, then cut right through to the other side. High-density foam can be cut into and carved out in finer detail. It is also less absorbent, so you get a smoother, less textured print. If you are stamping over a large area, you will find the stamp easier to use if you mount the foam on to a hardboard base and use wood glue to attach a small wooden door knob to the back. This will then act as a convenient handle for you to hold.

RIGHT: Commercial rubber stamps are available in designs to suit all tastes.

SURFACE FINISHES

When you print with stamps, the shape of the design remains constant but there are many different finishes that can be achieved. The factors affecting these are the surface that you stamp on to as well as the material used to make up the stamp, and the substance that you stamp with. All of these can vary enormously. To illustrate some of the possible effects that you can achieve, we have printed motifs with emulsion (latex) paint and then experimented with simple different finishes.

ALTERING EFFECTS

Once the pattern has been stamped on the wall (or on a wooden surface), there are various ways that you can alter its regular appearance. You can make the original print appear softer or darker using the following simple techniques. All you need is some abrasive paper (sandpaper) or tinted varnish.

1 This is the basic design. A foam rubber stamp was pressed into blue emulsion (latex) paint and printed on an emulsion-painted wall.

2 The print was allowed to dry and then it was lightly rubbed back using fine-grade abrasive paper (sandpaper).

3 This stamp has been darkened with a coat of tinted antiquing varnish. As well as protecting the surface, it deepens the colour and adds a slight sheen.

DEPTH EFFECTS

Varnish can be used over your designs to add depth to the colour and protect the wall surface. These prints, made with a polystyrene (Styrofoam) stamp, demonstrate the changes made by coats of varnish. Tinted varnish comes in many shades, and enriches the colour with each application.

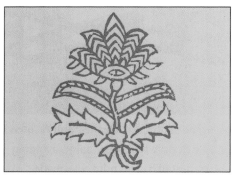

1 This is the basic stamped pattern in grey emulsion (latex) paint on a light buttermilk-coloured background.

2 This is the surface after one coat of tinted varnish was applied. It has deepened the yellow considerably.

3 A second coat of the same varnish was applied and the colour has turned deep pine-yellow.

WOOD APPLICATION

You can use most types of paint on wood, although some will need sealing with a protective coat of varnish. New wood needs to be sealed with a coat of shellac – this stops resin leaking through the grain. Below are some examples of rubber, sponge and potato prints made on wood with a variety of media. Woodstains, varnishes and paints have different properties and create different effects depending on the stamp used. The wood grain gives extra texture and interest to the stamped design.

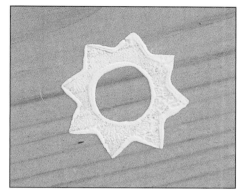

This example shows emulsion paint applied with a rubber stamp.

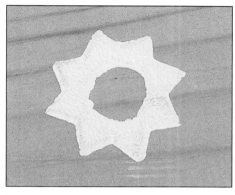

This print was made with emulsion paint applied with a sponge stamp.

This is an example of emulsion (latex) paint applied with a potato-cut.

This shows an example of woodstain applied with a rubber stamp.

This print was made with woodstain applied with a sponge stamp.

This is the effect of woodstain applied with a potato-cut.

This is an example of tinted varnish applied with a rubber stamp.

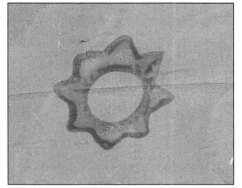

This print was made with tinted varnish applied with a potato-cut.

This shows an example of red ink applied with a potato-cut.

CERAMIC AND GLASS APPLICATION

Different surfaces bring out the different qualities of paint. The kind of stamp used will also have a big influence on the final result. To illustrate the different effects that can be achieved, we have used motifs cut from rubber, foam and potato, with a variety of inks, paints and stains. Some choices may seem unusual, like woodstain on terracotta, but experimentation can produce unexpected successes!

The print on this flowerpot was made with emulsion (latex) paint using a sponge.

This print was made with woodstain applied with a sponge.

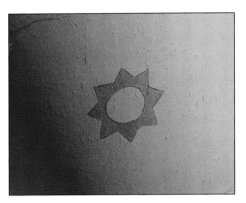

The print on this pot was made with tinted varnish using a rubber stamp.

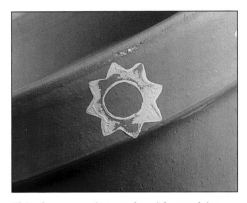

This shows a print made with emulsion paint applied with a rubber stamp.

This print was made with woodstain applied with a potato-cut.

This is an example of a print made with tinted varnish applied with a potato-cut.

These prints were made on a ceramic plate with acrylic enamel paint, applied with a potato-cut (top left), a sponge (top right), and a rubber stamp (bottom).

These glass prints were made with acrylic enamel paint thinned with clear acrylic varnish, using a sponge (top left), rubber stamp (top right) and potato-cut (bottom).

These prints were applied to glass with a coil of foam dipped into emulsion paint. The emulsion was left to dry, then covered with a protective coat of clear varnish.

TILE APPLICATION

These are just a small selection of the different effects that can be achieved by stamp printing on to tiles. Remember to clean the tiles thoroughly before decorating. We recommend that you always use acrylic enamel paints and, wherever possible, decorate them before you put them on a wall because this gives you the chance to add to their resilience by baking them in the oven. Always follow the manufacturer's instructions for times and temperatures, and ensure your tiles can withstand this treatment. You can create borders, overall patterns or individual highlights.

These little circles were made by dipping bored wine bottle corks into red and blue paint, and printing in rows.

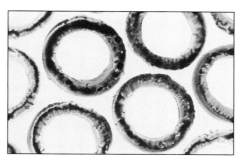

These larger circles were made using a potato-cut. The transparent effect comes from the potato starch mixing in with the paint.

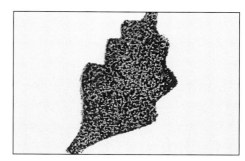

This print shows an example made with a shaped, medium-density sponge. The textured effect is due to the density of the sponge.

This pattern was made using small rubber stamps cut from an eraser. A zigzag pattern like this makes a good border.

This heart was cut from medium-density sponge. The textured effect is opaque but "powdery".

This pattern was made by dipping straight strips of high-density foam into red and blue paint. The thickness of the strips can be varied to produce a tartan pattern.

A small square of foam was used to print this chequerboard effect. This pattern is quite time-consuming, but very effective.

This high-density foam stamp was coloured with a brush to make a three-colour print. These make good highlights mixed in with single-colour prints.

This border was made with a medium-density foam block, printed in different colours. The edges must be aligned accurately for best effect.

THE PROJECTS

Home ornaments and accessories are probably the ideal starting-point if you have never considered a rubber stamp as a decorating tool. You can transform a lampshade, picture frame or wooden tray in minutes, with minimal effort and even less mess. All you need is a stamp and an inkpad to create an all-over pattern, then a quick rinse with water to clean the stamp. What could be easier? Starting a new craft activity is often the most difficult part, so it makes sense to begin with something small, until you have built up the confidence to attempt more ambitious projects. This shouldn't take long, because stamping is so easy and so little can go wrong.

ABOVE: A wide range of accessories are suitable for stamping, for example giftwrap, book covers, lampshades, as well as this cutlery rack.

LEFT: Most of the projects in this section use ready-made stamps. Printing on paper is particularly simple and inexpensive.

GOTHIC DISPLAY PLATE

Large china display plates look great mounted on the wall and they don't have to be confined to country kitchen-type interiors, as demonstrated by this bold pattern. The plate used here is a larger platter with a pale blue border outlined in navy blue, although the design can also be stamped on a plain plate. Use acrylic enamel paint to stamp on ceramics and glassware. It can be baked in a household oven according to the manufacturer's instructions. The resulting patterns are very hard-wearing and even seem to stand up to dishwashers and scouring pads, but the paints are recommended for display rather than for food use.

You will need

- black stamp pad
- diamond and crown stamps
- scrap paper
- scissors
- display plate
- acrylic enamel paint in navy blue and deep orange
- plates
- foam rollers
- ruler

1 Use the stamp pad to print eight diamond motifs and one crown on paper and cut them out. Arrange them on the plate to plan the design of the border pattern and central motif.

2 Spread some navy blue acrylic enamel paint on to a plate and run a roller through it until it is evenly coated. Ink the diamond stamp, then remove one of the paper shapes and stamp a diamond in its place.

OPPOSITE: Choose a display plate with a wide border and select a diamond stamp that will fit neatly inside it.

3 Place a ruler under the plate, so that it runs centrally from the printed motif to the one opposite. Line up the stamp with the edge of the ruler to print the second motif. Print diamond motifs on the other two sides of the plate in the same way, then fill in the diamonds in between, judging by eye.

4 Ink the crown stamp with deep orange paint and stamp a single crown in the centre of the plate. Bake the plate in the oven, following the paint manufacturer's instructions.

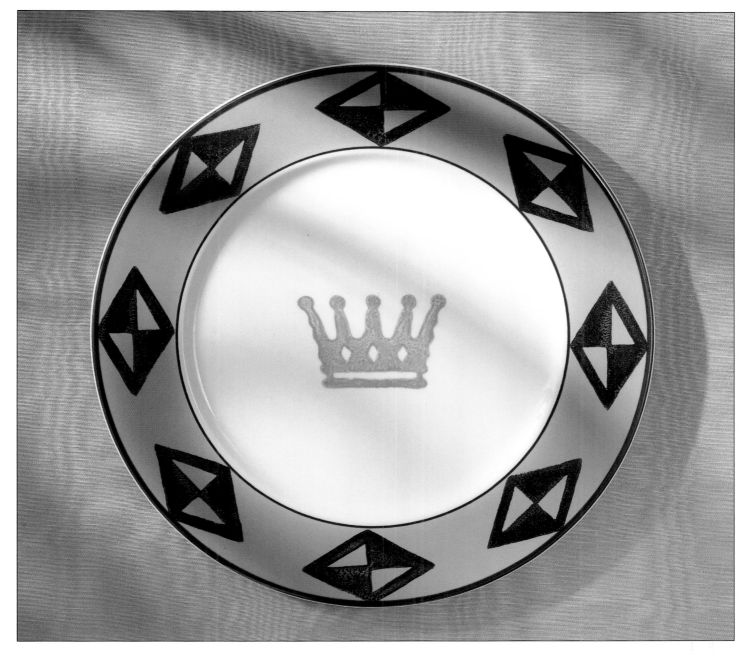

GRAPE JUG

Awhite ceramic jug like this one seems to be crying out for some stamped decoration, and the grape vine stamps do the trick in minutes. Choose a well-proportioned plain jug and transform it into something that is decorative as well as practical. Acrylic enamel paint is relatively new on the market and, although it resembles ordinary enamel, it is in fact water-based and does not require harmful solvents for cleaning brushes and stamps. Follow the manufacturer's instructions to "fire" the stamped jug in a domestic oven to add strength and permanence to the pattern. Without "firing", the paint will only stand up to non-abrasive cleaning.

You will need

- white ceramic jug (pitcher)
- detergent and clean cloth
- grape, tendril and leaf stamps
- black stamp pad
- scrap paper
- scissors
- acrylic enamel paint in black and ultramarine blue
- plate
- foam roller

1 Wash the jug in hot water and detergent, then wipe dry with a clean cloth to ensure that there is no grease on the surface.

2 Print a grape, a tendril and a leaf on to scrap paper and cut them out. Arrange them on the jug to plan the finished design.

3 Mix together the black and ultramarine blue acrylic enamel paint on a plate. Run the roller through the paint until it is evenly coated and ink the stamps. Stamp the motifs following your planned arrangement as a guide.

4 The leaf stamp may be used to fill any gaps, and the pattern may be repeated on the other side of the jug. Follow the manufacturer's instructions if you wish to make the design permanent by "firing" it in the oven.

RIGHT: For a more naturalistic effect, stamp the grapes in purple and the leaves and tendrils in green.

PERSONALIZED FLOWERPOTS

Commercially decorated flowerpots can be very expensive but you can customize ordinary clay pots very easily – and the designs will be uniquely yours. The sunwheel motif used here is an ancient symbol with real energy. The colours chosen create a vibrant display that is best complemented by bright, attractive pot plants. Change the plants according to the season or to suit your mood. Three stamps, three colours of paint and a roll of masking tape are all you need to turn plain flowerpots into a sensational display.

You will need

- pencil
- tracing paper
- fine-tipped pen
- craft knife
- spray adhesive
- high-density foam, such as upholstery foam
- acrylic enamel paint in navy blue, red and cream
- plates
- glazed and plain terracotta flowerpots
- masking tape

1 Trace, transfer and cut out the pattern shapes from the template section. Lightly spray the shapes with adhesive and place them on the foam.

2 Use a craft knife to cut around the outlines of the large sunwheel motif. Scoop out the background and the pattern details.

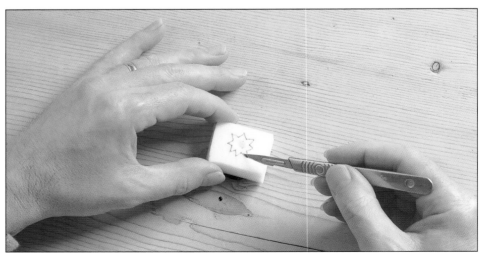

3 Cut out the small motif, then scoop out the centre circle in the same way as the large sunwheel motif.

4 Spread an even coating of navy blue acrylic enamel paint on to a plate and press the large sunwheel motif into it. Make a test print to make sure that the stamp is not overloaded.

5 Stamp the large motif around the flowerpot four times. If you are using a larger flowerpot, you will be able to fit in more prints.

6 Spread an even coating of red acrylic enamel paint on to a plate and press the small motif into it. Make a test print to make sure the stamp is not overloaded. Stamp the small motif in groups above and below the large ones.

7 Cut out a small stepped triangle from foam using a craft knife.

8 Place two parallel strips of masking tape around the top end of a blue-glazed flowerpot. Leave a 1cm/$\frac{1}{2}$in gap between the two strips.

9 Squeeze some cream acrylic enamel paint on to a plate. With an offcut of foam, apply the paint to the gap between the two strips of masking tape.

10 Allow time for the paint to dry, then peel off the masking tape to reveal the cream border around the top of the pot.

11 Make sure the cream paint is spread evenly on a plate. Press the stepped triangle shape into it. Make a test print first, then stamp the pattern above and below the cream line, matching up the points of the triangle.

RIGHT: Make a mix-and-match set of stamped flowerpots, using coloured glazed pots or plain terracotta ones. One of these flowerpots, planted with spring flowers or bulbs, would make a lovely home-made gift.

DECORATED TILES

These days you can buy wonderful decorated tiles in all shapes and sizes, but they cost a fortune! So, why not use stamps and paint to make your own set of exclusive decorated tiles? Acrylic enamel paint resembles ordinary enamel, but it is in fact water-based and does not include harmful solvents. If you are decorating loose tiles, bake them in a domestic oven following the manufacturer's instructions to "fire" the colour and give added strength and permanence. The fired tiles will be waterproof and resilient to non-abrasive cleaning. If you are stamping on to a tiled wall, it is best to position the design where it will not need too much cleaning – the paint will certainly withstand an occasional soaking and can be wiped with a damp cloth.

You will need

- plain off-white tiles
- detergent and clean cloth
- acrylic enamel paint in blue and green
- plates
- foam rollers
- small, large and trellis heart stamps

1 Wash the tiles with detergent and hot water, then dry them thoroughly with a clean cloth before you apply any paint. The tiles must be clean and grease-free.

2 Spread some blue paint on to the plate and run a roller through it until it is evenly coated. Ink the small heart stamp and print two hearts side by side at the top of the tile, with equal spacing on either side.

3 Align the next two stamps directly below the first. Take care not to smudge the first two when stamping the second row. Acrylic enamel paint dries fast, so you only need to wait a few minutes to avoid smudges.

4 To make another design, ink the large heart stamp and make a single print on another off-white tile. Press the stamp down, then lift it off immediately to get an interesting surface texture.

5 Ink the large heart stamp and print overlapping the edges, so that the point is at the top edge of the tile and the curved part is at the bottom.

6 Ink the large heart stamp and make a first print with the heart angled to the left. Leave it to dry, then print another heart angled to the right as shown.

7 Spread some green paint on to a plate and run a roller through it until it is evenly coated. Ink the trellis heart stamp and print a single heart in the centre of a tile.

8 Continue printing a single trellis heart in the centre of each tile. The texture will be different on every print, making the tiles look far more interesting and giving an expensive hand-painted effect.

RIGHT: If you prefer, stamp fewer tiles with the heart motifs and use them as individual highlights on a chequerboard pattern of plain tiles. See the Country Kitchen project for an example of how to position the stamped tiles.

COUNTRY KITCHEN

Specialist suppliers sell beautifully decorated tiles but they can be very expensive. Stamps and paint allow you to create unlimited designs for your tiles. The grape stamp is inked with two shades of green that blend in the middle in a slightly different way each time. Small touches such as the rustic hanging rail and the wooden plate add rustic authenticity to a country kitchen. The wood for the rail needs to be old and weathered. The nails banged into the rail as hangers are called "cut" nails, which are used for floorboarding. Attach the rail to the wall and hang fresh herbs from it, conveniently close to the cooker (stove). The wooden plate is stamped with different parts of the tendril motif to make a decorative border and central design.

You will need

- plain tiles
- detergent and clean cloths
- acrylic enamel paint in blue-green and yellow-green
- plates
- foam rollers
- grape, leaf and tendril stamps
- emulsion (latex) or acrylic paint in olive-green
- scrap paper
- weathered piece of wood, maximum 30cm/12in long
- long "cut" nails or hooks
- hammer or drill
- black stamp pad
- scissors
- wooden plate, sanded to remove any stain or varnish
- vegetable oil

1 Wash the tiles in hot water and detergent, then wipe dry to ensure that there is no grease on the surface.

2 Spread some blue-green acrylic enamel paint on to one plate and some yellow-green paint on to another. Run the rollers through the paint until they are evenly coated.

3 Ink the leaf stamp and the top and right side of the grape stamp with the blue-green roller. Ink the rest of the grape stamp with the yellow-green roller.

4 Stamp a bunch of grapes in the centre of each tile. Remove the stamp directly, taking care not to smudge the print. If you do make a mistake, you can simply wipe off the paint with a clean cloth and start again. Follow the manufacturer's instructions to "fire" the tiles in the oven if required.

5 For the hanging rail, spread some olive-green emulsion (latex) or acrylic paint on to a plate and run a roller through it until it is evenly coated. Ink the leaf stamp and stamp twice on to scrap paper to remove some of the paint.

6 Stamp on to the length of weathered wood without re-inking the stamp. The resulting print will be light and faded-looking, like the wood itself. Make as many prints as you can fit along the length. Hammer in the nails or drill and screw in the hooks to complete the hanging rail.

7 For the wooden plate, stamp several tendrils on to scrap paper using the black stamp pad and cut them out. Arrange them on the plate to work out the spacing and positioning of the motifs.

8 Spread some olive-green emulsion or acrylic paint on to a plate and run a roller through it until it is evenly coated. Ink the corner of the tendril stamp comprising the two curls that will make up the border pattern. Carefully begin stamping these motifs around the edge of the plate.

9 Ink the whole stamp and stamp two tendrils in the centre of the plate. Leave the paint to dry.

10 Dip a clean cloth into some vegetable oil and rub this into the whole surface of the plate, including the stamped pattern. You can repeat this process once all the oil has been absorbed into the wood. Each time you rub oil into the plate, the colour of the wood will deepen.

RIGHT: Stamp co-ordinating motifs on tiles and wooden accessories, using different paints and techniques appropriate to each surface. Position the grape tiles as highlights or create an all-over effect, as illustrated in the Decorated Tiles project.

STARRY VASE

The transparency of glass gives a new dimension to the stamped stars. The colour is applied to one surface, but the design is visible from all sides. You could try the stamps on any plain glass vase – this one was particularly easy to work with because of the flat surfaces. There are now some paints available called acrylic enamels. These are suitable for use on glass and ceramics and they give a hard-wearing finish that stands up to non-abrasive washing. The selection of colours is great, so take a look at them and try some glass stamping.

You will need

- glass vase
- detergent and clean cloth
- dark-coloured acrylic enamel paint
- plate
- foam roller
- large star stamp
- piece of glass

1 Wash the vase to remove any grease from the surface. Dry it thoroughly.

2 Spread some paint on to the plate and run the roller through it until it is evenly coated. Ink the stamp and make a test print on a piece of glass.

3 Stamp the stars randomly on to the glass vase. Apply gentle pressure with a steady hand and remove the stamp directly to avoid it sliding on the slippery surface.

FOLIAGE VASE

These stamped leaves will definitely add a designer touch to a plain glass vase, making it worthy of display with or without flowers or an arrangement of decorative leaves. The transparent glass allows the print to be seen from all sides, and the paint disperses on the smooth surface, adding texture to the leaves. Acrylic enamel paints are suitable for both glass and ceramics, and they have a consistency which works well with stamps. They also leave a glossy, hard-wearing finish that can be strengthened in an oven, if the manufacturer's instructions are followed carefully.

You will need

- plain rectangular glass vase
- detergent and clean cloth
- acrylic enamel paints in black and white
- plates
- foam rubber rollers
- leaf stamp

1 Wash the vase and wipe it dry with a clean cloth to ensure that there is no grease on the surface. Spread some black and white paint on to two plates. Run a roller through the white paint, and use it to ink the leaf stamp.

2 Print the first stamp on to the top half of the vase. Remove the stamp directly, taking care that it does not slide on the surface and smudge the print. If you make mistakes, they can be wiped off with a clean cloth.

3 Clean the leaf stamp and ink it with the black paint in the same way as with the white paint. Stamp a black leaf below the white one, so that it faces in the opposite direction. Allow to dry. If you wish to strengthen the paint in the oven, do so following the paint manufacturer's instructions.

HEARTS VASE

Take a plain vase and stamp it with rows of primary-coloured hearts to create a bright and cheerful display piece. Instead of being purely functional, the vase becomes artistic and decorative – this is one to put on the mantlepiece with or without cut flowers. There are now some paints available called acrylic enamels. These are suitable for use on glass and ceramics and they give a hard-wearing finish that stands up to non-abrasive washing. The selection of colours is great, so choose your own combination to suit the decor of your room.

You will need

- plain rectangular glass vase
- detergent and clean cloth
- acrylic enamel paints in yellow, blue and red
- plate
- foam roller
- small heart stamp

1 Wash the vase to remove any grease from the surface and dry it thoroughly. This will give you a better surface for stamping and will ensure a more successful print.

2 Spread a small amount of yellow paint on to the plate and run the roller through it until it is evenly coated. Ink the stamp and print a diagonal row of hearts on to the glass, starting at the top left-hand corner. Lift the stamp directly so that the prints are crisp and do not smudge.

3 Clean the stamp and ink it with blue paint. Add blue hearts in between the yellow ones as shown.

4 Clean the stamp and ink it with red paint. Then complete the design by adding the red hearts in the spaces left on the vase.

RIGHT: Repeating a simple motif in bright primary colours creates a very modern cheerful effect.

VALENTINE VASE

Present a dozen red roses in this beautiful stamped vase and you won't need Cupid's arrow to get your point across! There are a number of different types of glass paint on the market, but this vase is stamped with acrylic enamels, which work on glazed ceramics as well. The cupid is first stamped in cream, then painted over with a mottled white, achieved by dabbing paint on with a brush. A heart stencil is cut from card (stock) and used in combination with the cherub to complete the romantic valentine theme.

You will need

- pencil
- stencil card (stock) or plastic
- craft knife
- self-healing cutting mat
- plain rectangular glass vase
- acrylic enamel paint in red, cream and white
- plate
- foam roller
- stencil brush (optional)
- cherub stamp
- artist's paintbrush

1 Draw a heart shape on to a small piece of stencil card (stock) or plastic. Cut out the stencil with a craft knife on a self-healing cutting mat.

2 Position the heart stencil on the vase. Use red acrylic enamel paint and either the foam roller or the stencil brush to stencil the heart.

3 Spread some cream acrylic enamel paint on to a plate and run the roller through it until it is evenly coated. Ink the cherub stamp and make a print above the heart. Remove the stamp directly to prevent it from sliding. Use the artist's paintbrush to stipple a mottled coating of white paint over the cherub. Do not cover the whole print.

BLACK ROSE VASE

The transparency of this plain glass vase creates the illusion that the black rose is floating in mid-air, somewhere above the mantelpiece. Glass is an interesting surface to stamp on because it is so smooth that the paint disperses as soon as it is applied. It is a good idea to have a spare piece of glass handy so that you can practise your stamp before committing yourself to the final print. This way, you can find out how much paint you need to get the desired effect.

You will need

- glass vase
- detergent and clean cloth
- acrylic enamel paint in black
- plate
- foam roller
- large rose stamp
- piece of glass

1 Wash the vase to remove any grease from the surface, then dry it thoroughly with a clean cloth.

2 Spread some black paint on to the plate and run the roller through it until it is evenly coated. Ink the stamp and make a test print on the glass.

3 Stamp the black rose in the centre of the vase front. Apply gentle pressure with a steady hand and remove the stamp directly to avoid it sliding on the slippery surface. If you are not happy with the print, you can wipe it off before it begins to dry, clean the glass with a cloth and try again.

JAPANESE-STYLE VASE

Transform a plain glass vase with some chic calligraphic stamping. For this project, high-density foam was cut into strips, then dipped into acrylic enamel paint. The strips were then twisted into different shapes to make a series of quick prints. Don't make too many prints – the end result should look like an enlargement of a Japanese calligraphic symbol. The paint finish is tough enough to withstand gentle washing, but take care, because all unfired surface decoration such as this is prone to chipping and peeling.

You will need

- set square (triangle)
- felt-tipped pen
- high-density foam, such as upholstery foam, 25 x 10 x 5cm/10 x 4 x 2in
- craft knife
- plain rectangular glass vase
- detergent and clean cloth
- acrylic enamel paint in black
- plate

1 Using a set square and felt-tipped pen, draw lines 1cm/½in apart along the length of the foam.

2 Cut along the lines using a craft knife, then part the foam and cut all the way through it.

3 Clean the vase thoroughly with a clean cloth to remove any surface grease and dry it well.

4 Spread an even coating of paint on to a plate. Curl up a strip of foam and dip it into the paint.

5 Use both hands, positioned just above the glass surface, to curl the foam strip into an open-ended shape. When the curve looks right, press it on to the vase. Lift it off straight away to avoid any smudging.

6 Press a straight strip of foam into the paint, then use it to continue the line around the side of the vase.

7 Complete the calligraphic design with a series of these straight black lines. Use different width strips of foam if necessary. Applying the pressure unevenly will give a more authentic effect.

RIGHT: Simple strips and curls of foam make very effective stamps. They can also be used on a curved glass surface.

SNOWFLAKE STORAGE JARS

Almost every kitchen could do with the occasional facelift. Rather than pay for a completely new look, why not just cheer up your storage jars and give your kitchen a breath of fresh air? You can create a whole new atmosphere by stamping patterns on your jars with acrylic enamel paint. The finish is quite tough and will stand up to occasional gentle washing, but will not withstand the dishwasher. Choose a design that suits your kitchen, or copy the pattern for the motif used here.

You will need

- pencil
- tracing paper
- spray adhesive
- high-density foam, such as upholstery foam
- craft knife
- detergent and clean cloth
- glass storage jars
- acrylic enamel paint in white
- plate
- tile

1 Trace and transfer the pattern shape from the template section. Lightly spray the shape with adhesive and place it on the foam. Cut around the outline with a craft knife.

2 Cut horizontally into the foam to meet the outline cuts then remove the excess foam.

3 Clean the glass jars thoroughly with detergent and a cloth, then dry them well. This will remove any grease and will provide a better surface.

4 Spread an even coating of paint on to the plate. Press the stamp into it and make a test print on a tile to make sure that the stamp is not overloaded.

5 Holding the jar steady with your spare hand, press the foam stamp around the side of the jar.

6 Rotate the stamp 90 degrees and make a second print directly below the first. Continue in this way, alternating the angle of the stamp with each print. Cover the whole surface of the jar with the snowflake motifs.

RIGHT: A flexible foam stamp is ideal for printing on a rounded glass surface. Experiment with other simple shapes.

VINTAGE GLASS BOWL

Turn a plain glass bowl into an exquisite table centrepiece by stamping a white tendril pattern on the outside. Stamped glassware looks wonderful because the opaque pattern seems to intermingle as you look through the transparent glass. Another advantage is that you can see the stamp as the print is being made, which helps you to position it correctly and avoid overlaps and smudges. Glass painting has become popular recently and there are several brands of specialist glass paint available. Acrylic enamel paint has a good consistency for stamping and is water-based, allowing you to simply wipe it off and start again if you make a mistake.

You will need

- plain glass bowl
- detergent and clean cloth
- acrylic enamel paint in white
- plate
- foam roller
- tendril stamp

1 Wash the bowl in hot water and detergent, then wipe dry to ensure that there is no grease on the surface. Spread some white acrylic enamel paint on to the plate and run the roller through it until it is evenly coated.

2 Ink the tendril stamp and stamp the first row of prints around the base of the bowl. Remove the stamp directly, taking care that it does not slide or smudge the print. If you do make a mistake, wipe off the paint with a clean cloth and start again.

3 Turn the stamp the other way up to stamp the second row of motifs. Position the prints in between the tendrils on the first row, so that there are no obvious gaps in the design.

4 Stamp one more row with the stamp the original way up. Allow the stamp to overlap the edge of the bowl, so that most of the stem is left out. Leave the bowl to dry or "fire" it in the oven to fix the design, following the paint manufacturer's instructions.

BELOW: *The delicate tendril design would also look attractive in a pale shade of green for a more modern effect.*

GLORIOUS GIFTWRAP

If you want to make a gift extra special, why not print your own wrapping paper, designed to suit the person to whom you are giving the present? All you need is a selection of rubber stamps, inkpads or paint, and plain paper. Your home-made giftwrap will show that you really wanted to make the gift memorable. Stamped paper is great at Christmas when you need to wrap lots of presents at the same time. Your gifts will look very individual, particularly if you continue the motif on to the labels.

You will need

- plain paper
- rubber stamps in a variety of motifs
- stamp inkpads

1 To make a non-regimented design, like this clover-leaf pattern, first stamp at one edge of the paper. Then rotate the stamp in your hand to change the direction of each print. Continue stamping the design, judging the spacing by eye and printing the motifs close together. Re-charge the stamp with ink as required.

2 Turn the paper and continue stamping the shapes. The end result should have roughly an even amount of background to pattern.

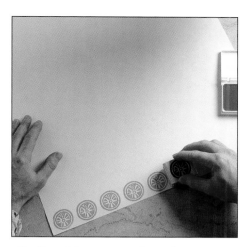

3 To achieve a more formal pattern, like this bird design, begin by stamping a row of shapes along the bottom edge.

4 Build up the design, alternating between two colours if you like, as shown here, to make an all-over pattern of closely spaced shapes.

RIGHT: Experiment with different motifs, repeating them to make all-over patterns. Try different kinds of paper, for example brown parcel wrap or tissue paper.

STARRY WRAPPING PAPER

Here is a way to print your own wrapping paper that will look better than any paper available in stores. The design will be unique and it hardly costs anything at all, unlike the hand-printed top-of-the-range designs available commercially. People have always enjoyed the satisfying activity of making repeat patterns, and nowadays we only really get a chance to do so at nursery school. But now you can grab some sheets of plain paper or colourful tissue paper, with a selection of bright paints to hand, clear the kitchen table and start stamping lots of different patterns.

You will need

- ruler
- pencil
- brown parcel wrap
- acrylic paint in brown, blue, white and cream
- plate
- foam roller
- starburst, folk-art and small star stamps

1 Use the ruler and pencil to mark one edge of the brown parcel wrap at approximately 12cm/5in intervals.

2 Spread a small amount of brown paint on to the plate and run the roller through it until it is evenly coated. Ink the starburst stamp and print on to the parcel wrap, using the pencil marks as a guide for the first row and judging the next rows by eye.

3 Ink the folk-art stamp with blue paint and stamp these stars in the spaces between the brown stars.

4 Ink the small star stamp with white paint and carefully fill in the centres of the blue stars.

ABOVE: Create your own designs using different star stamps. Use different colours for specific occasions, for example red and gold paints would be ideal for Christmas.

5 Stamp cream stars along diagonal lines between the rows of blue and brown stars.

CHRISTENING PARTY

The giftwrap, cards and table setting of this project will all help to make a traditional christening or naming-day party an unforgettable occasion. Use the cherubs to announce the baby's birth and herald the start of the celebrations. Buy a good-quality white paper for the cards. Some papers are deckle-edged, while others are textured. The choice is a personal one and a textured surface will give interesting stamped effects, so experiment on samples of paper. Set off the hand-printed wrapping paper by tying the parcels with white satin ribbons and bows.

You will need

- large white tablecloth or sheet
- backing card (stock)
- 1 swag and 2 cherub stamps
- fabric paint in bottle-green and silver
- plates
- foam rollers
- iron
- paper table napkins in white and bottle-green
- acrylic paint in bottle-green, white and blue-grey
- white notepaper
- scissors
- ruler
- pencil
- water-based size
- silver transfer leaf
- soft cloth
- fine wire (steel) wool
- silver wrapping paper
- newspaper
- black stamp pad
- scrap paper
- small strip of card

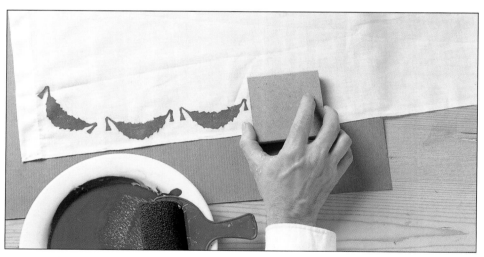

1 Lay the tablecloth or sheet on to the backing card (stock). Ink the swag stamp with bottle-green fabric paint and print across one corner of the cloth, so that the tassels are about 2.5cm/1in from the edges. Stamp swags all around the edge of the cloth to create a scalloped effect.

2 Spread some silver fabric paint on to a plate and run a roller through it until it is evenly coated. Ink both cherub stamps and, alternating the two designs, make a print above every other swag all around the edge of the cloth.

3 Continue to stamp a widely spaced cherub pattern in the centre of the cloth, alternating both stamps and rotating the direction of the prints. Follow the manufacturer's instructions to fix (set) the fabric paint with an iron.

4 For the napkins, spread some bottle-green acrylic paint on to a plate and run a roller through it until it is evenly coated. Ink the cherub stamps and make one print on each white table napkin.

5 Spread some white acrylic paint on to a plate. Use a roller to ink the cherub stamps. Stamp a white cherub on each green napkin.

6 To make the cards, cut and fold the paper to the required size, at least 14 x 11.5cm/5½ x 4½in. Draw pencil lines on the back of the stamp block to mark the mid-points on each side to help position the stamp accurately. Spread some blue-grey acrylic paint on to a plate and run a roller through it until it is evenly coated. Ink the stamp and print cherubs on the cards. Leave to dry.

7 Spread water-based size on to a plate and run a roller through it until it is evenly coated. Ink the cherub stamps with size and overprint the blue-grey prints. Leave to dry for the time recommended by the manufacturer until the size becomes tacky. Lay sheets of silver leaf on to the size and burnish the backing paper with a soft cloth.

8 Remove the backing paper and use wire (steel) wool to rub away excess silver leaf still clinging to the paper.

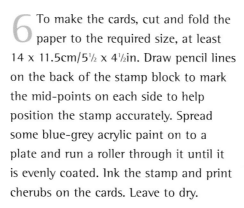

9 To make the wrapping paper, lay the silver paper on some newspaper on a flat surface. Using the black stamp pad, stamp several cherubs and swags on scrap paper and cut them out. Arrange the paper motifs on the silver paper to plan your design. Cut a card strip as a guide to the spacing between the motifs.

10 Spread some bottle-green acrylic paint on to a plate and run a roller through it until it is evenly coated. Ink the cherub stamp and print cherubs on the silver paper. Use the card strip to space the stamps.

11 Ink the swag stamp with white acrylic paint and print the linking swags between the cherub motifs.

RIGHT: Your guests will be delighted with hand-printed co-ordinating invitations and table linen for a special occasion such as a christening, wedding or silver wedding. For a golden wedding party, use gold fabric paint and gold wrapping paper.

BOHEMIAN BOOK COVERS

Brown parcel wrap is perfect book-covering material – it is strong, folds crisply and costs very little. The paper usually has a shiny side and a matt side, with the matt side more absorbent to paint. Pattern making with potato cuts is great fun, and the elements used here – a small solid square, a square outline, and a triangle – can be used in different combinations to make a variety of designs. Use the three paint colours to make your own design. These papers would make ideal covers for a row of cookbooks on a kitchen shelf. The watercolour paint is mixed with PVA (white) glue which dries transparent, leaving a slight sheen that looks great combined with the characteristic potato-cut texture.

You will need

- knife
- 2 potatoes
- bowl
- PVA (white) glue
- paintbrush
- watercolour paint in brick-red, brown and yellow-ochre
- plate
- craft knife
- brown parcel wrap

1 Cut the potatoes in half with a knife, then trim the edges to give them all the same square shape.

2 In a bowl mix PVA (white) glue and water in equal amounts, then add a drop of watercolour paint. The texture should be thick and sticky.

3 Spread an even coating of the paint mixture on to a plate then dip a potato into it – this will make it easier to see the design as you cut it out. Leave a square border around the edge of the potato shape, then divide the rest of the surface diagonally. Scoop out one triangular section with a craft knife.

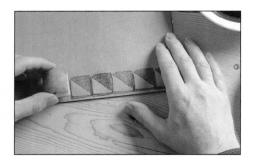

4 Print a row of this pattern along the bottom edge of the paper.

RIGHT: A humble potato cut can be repeated to build up sophisticated geometric designs and create a co-ordinating set of book covers.

5 Stamp the following row with the same stamp the other way up. Add variety to the design by rotating the stamp for each new row, to form different patterns.

6 To make a chequerboard pattern, leave a gap between the prints. Dip a small piece of potato into the paint and stamp dots in the middle of the blank squares. Experiment with your own combinations.

WEDDING ALBUM COVER

Custom-made wedding photograph albums are never as special as one you make yourself. For most of us, a wedding is the only time we are photographed professionally looking our very best, so the presentation should do the pictures justice. The album should have a solid spine, so don't choose the spiral-bound type. Visit a specialist paper dealer and discover the wonderful range of textured papers. The paper is stamped with gold size and gold leaf is laid on to it to create gleaming golden cherubs and swags. Initials or the date of the wedding add the finishing touch.

You will need

- large photograph album with a solid spine
- white textured paper
- scissors or craft knife
- double-sided tape
- cherub and swag stamps
- black stamp pad
- scrap paper
- gold size
- plate
- foam roller
- gold transfer leaf
- soft-bristled paintbrush
- gold transfer letters or fine artist's brush (optional)

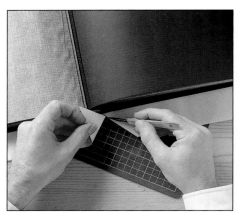

1 Lay the opened album on the sheet of paper and trim the paper to size. Allow a border round the edges to fold over the paper inside the cover. Cover the album with the paper, sticking down the overlaps on the inside of the cover.

2 Stamp several cherubs and swags on scrap paper and cut them out. Lay them out on the album cover with any initials or dates to plan your design. When you are happy with the design, use the paper cut-outs as a guide for positioning the stamps.

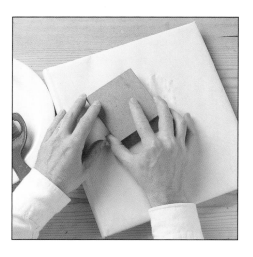

3 Spread some gold size on to the plate and run the roller through it until it is evenly coated. Ink the stamps with size and stamp the design on the album cover. Leave to dry for the time recommended by the manufacturer until the size becomes tacky.

5 Stamp a bunch of grapes on to a small piece of brown parcel wrap. Carefully cut around the outline with a craft knife on a self-healing cutting mat to make a stencil.

6 Spread some off-white paint on to a plate and run a roller through it until it is evenly coated. Position the stencil on a notebook cover and run the roller over the stencil to make a solid grape shape. Leave to dry.

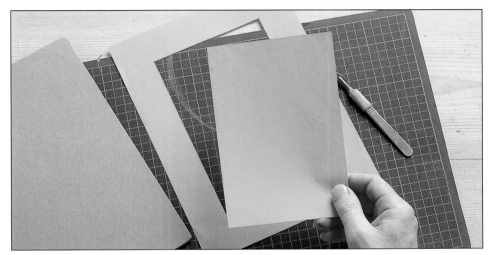

7 Ink the grape stamp with sepia acrylic paint and overprint the stencilled shape to add the detail.

8 For the folder, cut a window out of a sheet of scrap paper the same size as the folder cover to make a paper frame.

9 Lay the window frame on the cover. Ink the leaf stamp with sepia paint and stamp leaves all over the cover, overlapping the frame. Leave to dry, then remove the frame to reveal a plain border around the leaf pattern.

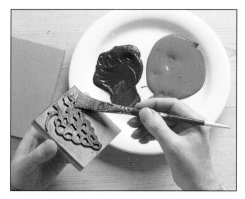

10 Mix some off-white paint into the sepia to make a lighter brown. Using a brush, apply the lighter brown paint to one side of the grape stamp and sepia to the other.

11 Stamp a single bunch of grapes on to the cover of a small file. The bunch of grapes will be shaded on one side, creating an interesting three-dimensional effect.

12 Place the folded cards of handmade paper on sheets of scrap paper. Stamp an all-over pattern of sepia tendrils, overlapping the edges so that the cards look as if they have been cut from a larger sheet of stamped paper. The texture of the paper will show through in places and the colour will vary as the paint gradually wears off the stamp, adding to the rich, handmade effect.

RIGHT: Once you realize how easy it is to make stamped stationery, notebooks and folders, there will be no turning back. For example, you could also print the grape stamp at the top of sheets of notepaper.

HERALDIC STATIONERY

Design and print a personalized set of stationery to add a touch of elegance to all your correspondence. Heraldic motifs have been used for centuries to decorate letters and secret diaries, but it is no longer necessary to live in a palace to be able to use them. This project demonstrates the variety of ways in which a single stamp can be used to produce different effects. The resulting stationery is based on a common theme but with plenty of individual flourishes. Experiment with your favourite colour combinations and try all-over or border patterns to add even more variety. Many craft shops sell special embossing powders that can be heated to produce a raised print.

You will need

- dark blue artist's watercolour paint
- plates
- foam rollers
- diamond, fleur-de-lys and crown stamps
- brown parcel wrap
- craft knife
- self-healing cutting mat
- small notebook, folder, postcards and textured and plain white notepaper
- gold paint
- dark blue paper
- ruler
- set square (triangle)
- paper glue
- fine artist's paintbrush

1 Spread some dark blue watercolour paint on to a plate and run a roller through it until it is evenly coated. Ink the diamond stamp and print one motif on to a small piece of the brown parcel wrap.

2 Cut out the diamond shape with a craft knife on a self-healing cutting mat. Try not to over-cut the corners because the shape will be used as a stencil and the paint may bleed through.

3 Position the paper stencil in the middle of the notebook cover and use the roller to apply dark blue watercolour paint through it. Leave to dry.

4 Spread some gold paint on to a plate and run the roller through it until it is evenly coated. Ink the diamond stamp and stamp a gold print directly over the solid blue diamond, lining up the edges as closely as possible.

5 Cut a rectangle the size of the fleur-de-lys stamp block out of dark blue paper. Measure and divide it in half lengthways. Cut away one side with a craft knife, leaving a narrow border around the edge to make a window in one side.

6 Using a ruler and set square (triangle) to position the stamp, print a dark blue fleur-de-lys in the centre of the folder. Glue the blue paper over the print so that half the fleur-de-lys motif shows through the window.

7 Ink the fleur-de-lys stamp with gold paint. Cover the cut-out side of the design with a straight-edged piece of parcel wrap. Stamp a gold fleur-de-lys to align with the sides of the blue print. Remove the piece of parcel wrap to reveal the final design, which will be half gold and half blue.

8 Stamp a blue fleur-de-lys on a notebook cover or postcard. Cover one half of it with a straight-edged piece of parcel wrap and overprint in gold to make a two-colour print.

9 Fold a piece of textured notepaper to make a card. Stamp a blue fleur-de-lys on the front of the card. The texture of the paper will show through in places. Add flourishes of gold paint using a fine artist's paintbrush.

10 Stamp a gold crown at the top of textured and plain white sheets of notepaper.

RIGHT: Experiment with other stamps and colours to create your own personalized stationery.

BOOK COVERS AND SECRETS BOX

This project evokes another era, when time passed by more slowly and leisure had nothing to do with aerobic exercise. Diaries and scrapbooks were kept and lovingly covered with printed papers and secret mementoes were hidden in locked wooden caskets. Recapture the spirit of a bygone age by stamping patterned papers and using them to bind sketchbooks, albums and diaries. Preserve the battered antiquity of an old wooden box by stamping it and lining it in muted shades of red and green, then rubbing back the paint to simulate years of wear and tear.

You will need

- black ink stamp pad
- tulip, leaf and pineapple stamps
- scrap paper
- scissors
- sugar (construction) paper
- ready-mixed watercolour paint in a droppered bottle in deep red, leaf-green and black
- plates
- long ruler
- diary, photo album or book, such as a sketchbook
- PVA (white) glue
- black bookbinding tape
- self-healing cutting mat
- craft knife
- old wooden box
- emulsion (latex) or acrylic paint in brick-red and sage-green
- foam roller
- wooden batten (furring strip)
- lining brush
- fine-grade abrasive paper (sandpaper) or wire (steel) wool
- furniture polish and soft cloth (optional)

1 For the book cover, use the stamp pad to print four tulips on scrap paper. Cut them out and arrange them in a row along the top edge of the sugar (construction) paper, side by side and alternately facing up and down. Use these paper prints as a guide for stamping.

2 Spread some deep red watercolour paint on to a plate and dip the stamp into it. Lay the ruler across the paper and use to align the stamp to print the first row. Re-ink the stamp after three prints for an irregular hand-printed effect.

3 Move the ruler down the width of a stamp block for each new row. Stamp the rows so that the tulips lie between the prints in the previous row. Cover the paper completely and leave to dry. Print more sugar paper, using the leaf and pineapple stamps and the leaf-green and black paint.

4 Cover the books with the stamped paper, sticking down any mitred corners with PVA (white) glue. Place a strip of bookbinding tape along the spine to cover the paper edges so there is an equal width of tape on the front and back cover. Trim away the tape at the top and bottom with a craft knife.

5 For the secrets box, use the stamp pad to print some tulips and leaves on scrap paper and cut them out. Arrange them on the wooden box to plan your design, deciding which motifs will be red and which green.

6 Spread some brick-red emulsion (latex) or acrylic paint on to a plate and run the roller through it until it is evenly coated. Ink the stamps and remove one paper shape at a time to stamp a leaf or tulip motif in its place.

7 Ink the leaf stamp with sage-green paint and stamp green leaves on the secrets box in the same way.

8 Place the wooden batten (furring strip) along the edge of the box and use the sage-green paint and the lining brush to paint an outline around the box and corner motifs. Slide your hand along the batten to keep an even line.

9 Leave the paint to dry completely, then lightly distress the stamped prints with abrasive paper (sandpaper) or wire (steel) wool. The secrets box can then be polished with furniture polish, if desired.

RIGHT: Sugar paper makes an effective background to the "distressed", aged stamp designs and is the ideal weight for book covers. If sugar paper is not readily available, you could use brown parcel wrap.

TREASURE BOXES

Sets of lidded round boxes made from lightweight wood, card (stock) or papier-mâché are often imported from the Far East and are readily available in the stores. The plain ones, sometimes called blanks, are not expensive and they make the ideal base for some imaginative stamping work. The hearts in this project have been grouped to form a larger motif, with some of them only partially stamped, so they don't look like hearts. As you can see, experimentation produces all sorts of variations on the heart theme.

1 Paint the lid of the box light grey with emulsion (latex) or acrylic paint. Leave to dry. If extra coverage is needed, apply more than one coat, leaving to dry between coats.

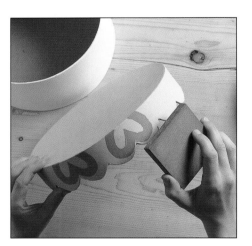

2 Spread some orange paint on to the plate and run the roller through it until it is evenly coated. Then ink the large heart stamp. Print the top half of the hearts around the side of the lid. Do not print the hearts too closely together – use the stamp to estimate the spacing before you begin.

3 Align the stamp with the pattern printed on the side of the lid, then print the pointed part of each heart around the top of the lid. This gives the impression that the hearts have been folded over the lid.

5 Still using the orange paint, stamp one complete large heart in the centre of the lid. Ink the small stamp with black paint and stamp a circle of hearts with their points radiating outwards between the yellow "V" shapes.

4 Use the same pointed part of the heart to print a zigzag border around the bottom edge of the box.

BELOW: *It is amazing how many different patterns can be created using a couple of simple motifs.*

MATISSE PICTURE FRAME

You can create instant art by combining stamp leaf prints with blocks of bright colour on a picture frame. Matisse's stunning cut-outs were the inspiration for this project. In his later life, Matisse used paper cuttings to create collage pictures that are as bold and fresh today as when they were first made. For the framed image, print a single leaf on to paper and enlarge it on a photocopier. Print it on to coloured paper and make a simple cut-out.

You will need

- broad wooden picture frame
- emulsion (latex) paint in black
- paintbrush
- set square (triangle)
- pencil
- artist's acrylic, gouache or poster paints in lime-green and fuchsia
- plate
- foam roller
- leaf stamp
- clear matt (flat) varnish and brush

1 Paint the frame in black (latex) emulsion and let it dry. Use a set square (triangle) and pencil to mark four squares in the corners of the frame, with sides the same as the width of the wood.

2 Paint the corner squares lime-green. You will need to apply several coats of paint for the most intense colour. Make sure that none of the black background shows through the lime-green.

3 Spread some fuchsia paint on to a plate and run the roller through it until it is evenly coated. Ink the leaf stamp and stamp one leaf in each lime-green corner. Rotate the stamp each time, so that the stem of the leaf always points inwards.

ABOVE: This work of art is surprisingly easy to achieve. Matisse's cut-outs will give you other ideas for colour schemes.

4 Let the paint dry, then apply a coat of clear matt (flat) varnish to seal and protect the picture frame.

STARRY PICTURE FRAME

This project combines many of the creative possibilities of stamping. It involves four processes: painting a background, stamping in one colour, overprinting in a second colour and rubbing back to the wood. These processes transform a plain wooden frame and they are neither time-consuming nor expensive. It is surprisingly difficult to find small, old frames that are broad enough to stamp. Fortunately, a wide range of basic, cheap frames can be found in do-it-yourself stores.

You will need

- picture frame
- emulsion (latex) paint in sky-blue, red-brown and gold
- paintbrush
- plate
- foam roller
- small and large star stamps
- fine wire (steel) wool or abrasive paper (sandpaper)

1 Paint the picture frame with sky-blue emulsion (latex) paint and leave it to dry thoroughly.

2 Spread a small amount of red-brown paint on to the plate and run the roller through it until it is evenly coated. Ink the small star stamp and print it in the middle of each side.

3 Using the red-brown paint, stamp a large star over each corner of the frame. Leave to dry thoroughly.

4 Ink the large stamp with gold paint and overprint the red-brown corner stars. Leave to dry before rubbing the frame gently with wire (steel) wool or abrasive paper (sandpaper) to give it a slightly aged appearance.

BELOW: Experiment with other stamps, choosing one to suit the frame. Large stars overlap the sides of this deep frame.

GRAPE PICTURE FRAME

A decorated frame draws attention to the picture within, while providing another opportunity to add colour and pattern to a room. This frame can be hung with the broad end at either the top or the bottom, depending on the nature of the picture it surrounds. The balance of the grape, leaf and tendril motif is reinforced by using the same colours to paint the border lines. Practise using a long-bristled lining brush on paper first before you paint the fine lines on the frame. The "hands-on" style does not require perfection – slightly wavy lines add character.

You will need

- grape, leaf and tendril stamps
- black stamp pad
- scrap paper
- scissors
- picture frame, painted brick-red with an olive-green border
- set square (triangle)
- pencil
- emulsion (latex) or acrylic paint in olive-green and ultramarine blue
- plate
- foam roller
- long-bristled lining brush
- damp cloth (optional)

1 Stamp all three motifs on to scrap paper and cut them out. Position them on the broad end of the picture frame to plan your design.

2 Use a set square (triangle) and pencil to draw a line around the frame, just inside the green border. Draw a second line around the centre of the frame.

3 Spread some olive-green paint on to one side of the plate and blue on to the other. Run the roller through the paint until it is evenly coated, allowing the colours to blend slightly in the middle. Ink the stamps and print the motifs in the planned positions.

4 Use the lining brush to paint the pencil lines ultramarine blue. Steady your hand by sliding it along the raised border as you work. If you make a very obvious mistake, wipe off the paint immediately with a damp cloth, but you may need to touch up the background colour when the new line has dried.

RIGHT: Choose stamp motifs and a colour scheme to complement your favourite picture.

SEEDPOD LAMPSHADE

Unusual lampshades can be very expensive. The solution is to take a plain lampshade and apply some surface decoration that will transform it from a utility object into a stylish focal point. This design, which resembles a seedpod, is easy to cut from high-density foam. It makes a bold, sharp-edged print and the flexibility of the foam means that it can bend around the curved surface. Remember to extend the pattern beyond the edges of the lampshade, so that only parts of the motifs appear. The lampshade will look as if it has been made from hand-printed fabric.

You will need

- pencil
- tracing paper
- spray adhesive
- high-density foam, such as upholstery foam
- craft knife
- thinned emulsion (latex) paint in creamy yellow and pale blue
- plates
- small rubber roller
- plain-coloured lampshade

1 Trace and transfer the seedpod pattern shape from the template section. Lightly spray the shape with adhesive and place it on the foam. Cut out the motif using a craft knife. Cut around the outline first, going all the way through the foam. Cut around the centre detail to a depth of about 1cm/½in, then under-cut and scoop out this section, and cut away the background.

2 Spread some creamy yellow paint on to a plate and coat the roller evenly. Use it to apply a coating of paint to the stamp.

3 Make the first print a partial one, using only the top end of the stamp. Continue to print at random angles, leaving plenty of spaces for the second colour. Wash the stamp, removing all traces of yellow paint.

BELOW: The outline shape looks like a stencil, but it is in fact all part of the home-made foam stamp.

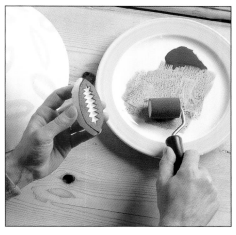

4 Spread some pale blue paint on a second plate and coat the roller. Use it to apply an even coating of paint to the stamp.

5 Stamp blue shapes at random angles in between the yellow ones. Be sure to make some partial prints so that the pattern continues over the edges.

FLORAL LAMPSHADE

A new lampshade can work wonders, freshening up a dull corner and providing as much in the way of style as in illumination. This paper shade has a good shape with interesting punched edges. However, a plain shade would work equally well for this project. In this design it is essential to space the rose pattern accurately, so make a quick paper pattern to ensure perfect results with every print.

You will need

- emulsion (latex) or fabric paint in pink and green
- plate
- 2 square-tipped paintbrushes
- large rose stamp
- scrap paper
- scissors
- masking tape
- plain lampshade (either paper or cloth)

1 Spread some pink and green paint on to the plate. Using the square-tipped paintbrushes, ink the leaves of the rose stamp green and the flower pink. (If one colour mixes with the other, just wipe them off and re-ink the stamp.)

2 Print five rose motifs on to scrap paper and cut them out.

3 Using masking tape, stick the paper roses round the lampshade. Make sure that they are spaced the same distance apart and not too close together. Depending on the size of the shade, you should be able to fit four or five roses round it.

4 Re-ink the stamp and lift off each paper rose individually as you stamp on to the lampshade itself. Hold the lampshade firmly with your spare hand and roll the stamp across the curved surface to get an even print.

RIGHT: This classic rose image is timeless and ever popular. It could be used on all kinds of projects.

STARFISH LAMPSHADE

This project transforms a plain, ordinary lamp into an individual and stylish accessory. Buy the cheapest lamp you can find because, once the base has been painted and the shade stamped, you won't be able to recognize the item you bought originally. The deep red stamps on the pink background not only give out a lovely coloured glow when the lamp is switched on, but cheer up a dull corner even when switched off.

You will need

◆ lamp with fabric shade and wooden base
◆ emulsion (latex) paint in deep red and light grey-blue
◆ paintbrush
◆ plates
◆ pencil
◆ foam roller
◆ starfish stamp

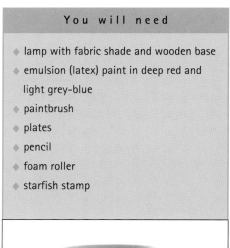

1 Paint the base of the lamp with deep red emulsion (latex) paint and leave to dry thoroughly.

2 Using a dry brush and a small amount of light grey-blue paint, lightly brush on the colour to shade the shape of the turned wood.

3 Use the stamp block to work out the spacing of the starfish round the shade. Lightly mark the design in pencil. Spread some deep red paint on to a plate and run the roller through it until it is evenly coated. Ink the stamp and begin by printing the bottom row of the pattern, following the pencil marks.

4 Stamp a row of starfish around the top of the shade. Remember to check the spacing as you go – you will fit fewer around the top than the bottom.

ABOVE: Simple stamping on the lampshade is given extra interest by painting and overpainting the base in two colours. Choose a colour scheme to suit your room.

FOLK COFFEE CANISTER

Rescue an old kitchen canister and give it a new identity as a piece of folk art. Painted tinware was very popular with early American settlers, and for years peddlers roamed the countryside loaded down with brightly painted cans, pitchers and bowls they sold from door to door. All these years later tinware is still a popular way of brightening up kitchen shelves. Prepare this canister by rubbing down the old paint with abrasive paper (sandpaper) to provide a surface for a fresh coat of emulsion (latex) paint. After stamping, bring out the colour and protect the surface with several coats of clear varnish.

You will need

- empty coffee canister
- abrasive paper (sandpaper)
- small household paintbrush
- emulsion (latex) paint in brick-red, black and bright red
- fine artist's paintbrushes
- plates
- foam roller
- tulip stamp
- clear gloss varnish and brush

1 Sand the canister. Paint the canister and lid brick-red. Leave to dry, then paint the rim of the lid black using a fine artist's paintbrush.

2 Run the roller through the black paint until it is evenly coated. Ink the tulip stamp and print a tulip on the side of the canister, tilting the stamp block around the curve of the canister.

3 Fill in the tulip shape carefully, using bright red paint and a fine artist's paintbrush.

ABOVE: *Stamping works well on tin surfaces. In this project, the tulip shape is filled in using a fine artist's paintbrush.*

4 Apply several coats of gloss varnish to seal and protect the canister. Allow each coat to dry completely before applying the next.

VINE LEAF CUTLERY RACK

A small wooden cutlery rack like this one provides another ideal surface for stamping. Use the stamps to loosely co-ordinate your kitchen or dining room without being swamped by matching patterns and colours. The wood has been stained blue and is then rubbed back to reveal some of the natural grain underneath. The two colours of the pattern are stamped separately using thinned emulsion (latex) paint for a light and airy finish.

BELOW: This design would look very attractive stamped on the top of a pine shelf unit or kitchen dresser.

1 Sand the surface of the cutlery rack to reveal some of the grain. Spread some dark olive-green paint on to a plate and thin it with water until it is a runny consistency.

2 Use the roller to ink the leaf stamp. Print two leaves side by side on the back and front of the rack as shown. Print two leaves one above the other on the sides. Leave to dry.

3 Spread some light olive-green paint on to a plate and run the roller through it until it is evenly coated. Ink just the tips of the leaves and overprint all the darker green prints. If some of the prints are slightly off-register, this will only add to the rustic appearance of the cutlery rack.

CANDLE BOX

A long time ago every home would have had a candle box hanging on the kitchen wall, kept full to meet the lighting needs of the household. Although rarely needed in quite the same way today, candle boxes are still popular and add to a comfortable atmosphere. Candle boxes can be bought, but are quite easy to make from five pieces of wood. The open top allows you to see when your supply is running low and the sight of the new candles is somehow reassuring as well as attractive.

You will need

- wooden candle box
- fine-grade abrasive paper (sandpaper)
- shellac and brush
- dark oak woodstain
- plate
- foam roller
- diamond, crown and fleur-de-lys stamps
- lining brush

1 Sand away any varnish and smooth any rough edges on the box.

2 Paint the bare wood with a single coat of shellac.

BELOW: *This box has a heraldic theme.*

3 Spread some woodstain on to a plate and run the roller through it until it is evenly coated. Ink the stamps and print a single motif on each side of the box. Print the fleur-de-lys so it will be visible above the candles. Use the lining brush to paint a thin border on all sides of the box.

WOODEN WINE CRATE

Old wood usually looks best with a faded rather than freshly painted pattern. The grape design here does not detract from the crate's rustic quality because it has been stamped in a muted green, then rubbed back to blend with the existing lettering on the wood. If you are lucky enough to find a custom-made wine crate like this one, it will simply need a good scrubbing with soapy water, then be left to dry before you stamp it.

You will need

- old wine crate or similar wooden box
- scrubbing brush (optional)
- emulsion (latex) paint in olive-green
- plate
- foam roller
- grape stamp
- fine abrasive paper (sandpaper)

1 If necessary, scrub the wine crate or box well with soapy water and a scrubbing brush. Leave the wood to dry.

2 Spread some olive-green paint on to a plate and run the roller through it until it is evenly coated. Ink the stamp and begin stamping a random pattern of grapes. Stamp at different angles to add variety.

3 Cover all the surfaces of the crate or box, overlapping the edge if the planks are too narrow to take the whole motif.

ABOVE: *Look out for a wooden crate or box with plenty of character. Your local wine merchant may be able to help.*

4 Leave the paint to dry, then rub back the pattern with abrasive paper (sandpaper) so that it becomes faded and blends with the original surface decoration or lettering. Rub gently and aim for a patchy, distressed appearance.

GILDED TRAY

This simple wooden tea tray is transformed into an item of historic grandeur by using an easy gilding technique. Begin by sanding away any old paint or varnish and painting the base of the tray in black and the sides in red-ochre emulsion (latex) paint, applying two or three coats. The heraldic motifs make up a central panel design, and the fine outline is repeated around the edge of the tray. The tray is stamped twice, first with the red-ochre paint and then with gold size, which is a transparent glue used for gilding. Dutch metal leaf is then applied over the size.

You will need

- wooden tea tray, prepared as above
- ruler
- pencil
- fleur-de-lys and diamond stamps
- black stamp pad
- scrap paper
- scissors
- emulsion (latex) paint in red-ochre
- plates
- foam roller
- thin wooden batten (furring strip)
- lining brush
- gold size and brush
- Dutch metal leaf
- soft and hard paintbrushes
- shellac and brush

1 Measure out and mark in pencil the six-sided central panel. Draw a border around the edge of the tray. Print eight fleurs-de-lys and five diamonds on to scrap paper and cut them out. Use them to plan your design, marking the base point of each motif in pencil on the tray. Spread some red-ochre paint on to a plate and run the roller through it until it is evenly coated. Ink the stamps and print the fleur-de-lys and diamond pattern.

2 Using the wooden batten (furring strip) to support your hand, use the lining brush and the red-ochre paint to paint a fine line around the design, following the pencil lines of the central panel. Paint another fine line just inside the edge of the tray. If you have never used a lining brush, practise making lines on scrap paper until you are confident with the technique.

3 Paint the sides of the tray with size. Leave the size to become tacky, according to the time specified by the manufacturer. Place one sheet of Dutch metal leaf on to the size at a time and burnish with the back of a soft brush. Spread the gold size on to a plate and use the roller to ink the stamps with size. Overprint the red-ochre patterns, stamping each print slightly down and to the left of the already printed motif to create a dropped shadow effect. Leave the size to become tacky and gild with Dutch metal leaf in the same way as before. Use a stiff paintbrush to sweep away the excess leaf. Seal the whole tray with a protective coat of shellac.

BELOW: This opulent treatment would also transform a plain wooden side table in a medieval-inspired drawing room.

TULIP TRAY

Paint and stamp a tray like this one and you will be tempted to display it rather than put it to practical use. You can in fact do both, if you apply several coats of varnish to give the tray a washable surface. The tulips and leaves are stamped on bold geometric shapes to give them added impact. The colours used here are not typical of folk art and give the tray a dramatic, contemporary look. You could use a more traditional colour combination, such as black, red and green, for a completely different effect.

You will need

- wooden tray
- emulsion (latex) paint in dusky blue, buttermilk-yellow and dark blue
- household paintbrushes
- ruler
- pencil
- plate
- foam roller
- tulip and leaf stamps
- clear satin varnish and brush

1 Paint the tray with dusky blue emulsion (latex) paint and leave to dry. Use a ruler and pencil to draw a square in the centre of the tray, then draw a square on the diagonal inside it. Add two rectangular panels on either side of the central square. The size of the panels will depend on the tray.

2 Paint the diagonal square and the two rectangles in buttermilk-yellow, and the remaining area of the larger square in dark blue. If your tray has cut-out handles, paint inside them in dark blue.

ABOVE: *Cheerful colours and bold shapes make a breakfast tray or television supper tray a pleasure to use. Choose a tray with high sides like this one.*

3 Spread some dark blue paint on to a plate and use the roller to ink the tulip and leaf stamps. Print two leaves on the side panels and two tulips in the central square, both end to end.

4 Apply at least three coats of clear satin varnish, allowing each coat to dry thoroughly before applying the next. The stamping will become more resistant with each coat of varnish.

TEMPLATES

The templates on the following pages may be resized to any scale required. The simplest way of doing this is to enlarge them on a photocopier, or trace the design and draw a grid of evenly spaced squares over your tracing. Draw a larger grid on another piece of paper and copy the outline square by square. Draw over the lines to make sure they are continuous.

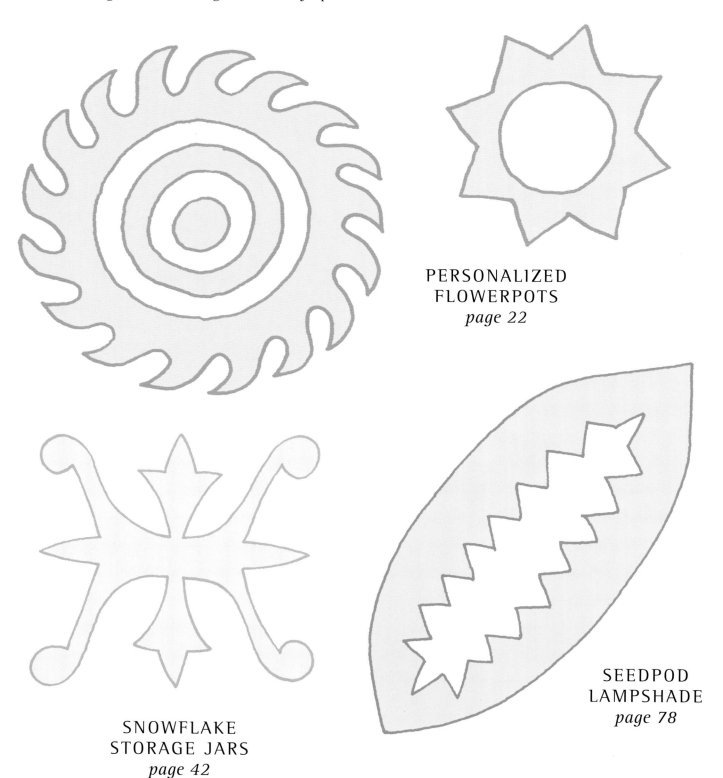

**PERSONALIZED
FLOWERPOTS**
page 22

**SNOWFLAKE
STORAGE JARS**
page 42

**SEEDPOD
LAMPSHADE**
page 78

INDEX